SLEEP MEDICINE

for kids

First paperback edition May 2024

Book design by Betty Nguyen & Brandon Pham

ISBN 978-1-957557-29-8 (paperback)

Printed in the United States of America

Published by Black Phoenix Press

www.mdforkids.org

To the friends and family who have supported and loved us unconditionally, and to the mentors who have guided and taught us more than we could have imagined:

Thank you.

Betty & Brandon

Sleep Medicine

(sleep MEH-duh-sn)

the branch of medicine concerned with the study, diagnosis, and treatment of sleep disorders

Sleep is a vital part of our daily routine that allows our body and brain to rest and recharge.

Non-rapid eye movement (NREM) sleep

Rapid eye movement (REM) sleep

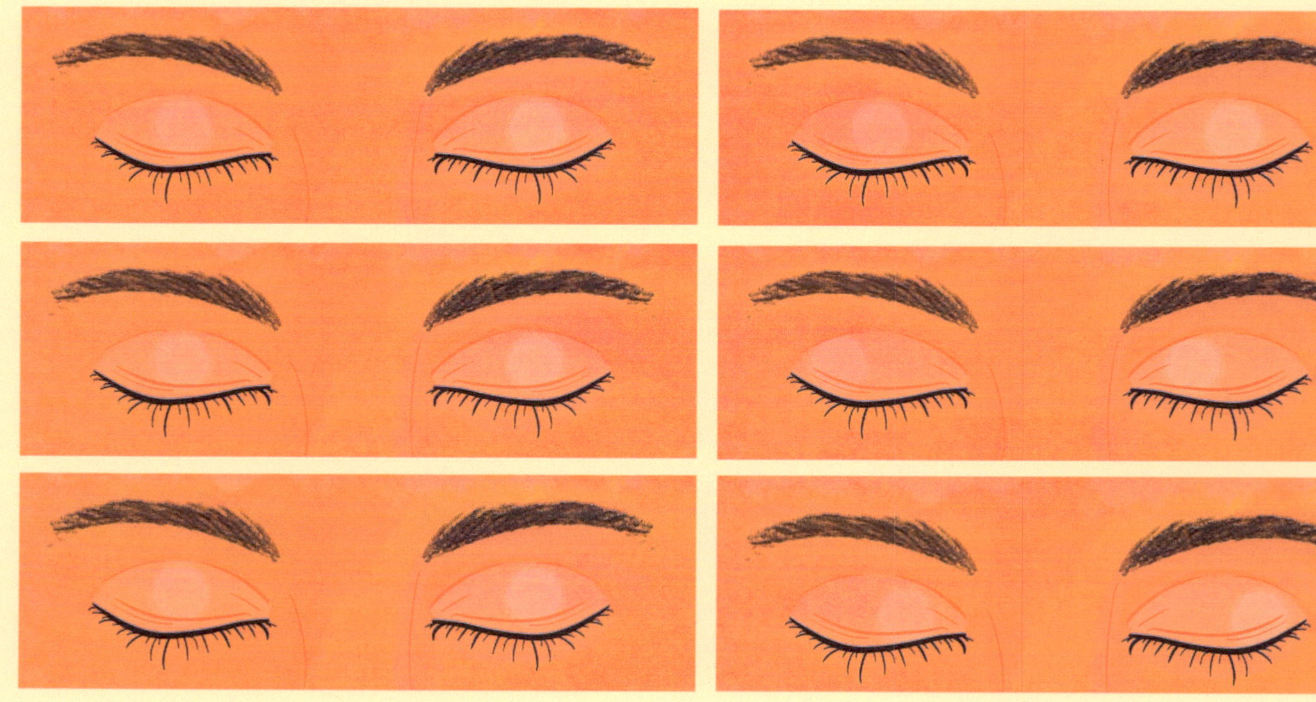

Eyes do not move under eyelids

Eyes move under eyelids

Sleep consists of two different phases: **non-rapid eye movement (NREM)** sleep and **rapid eye movement (REM)** sleep.

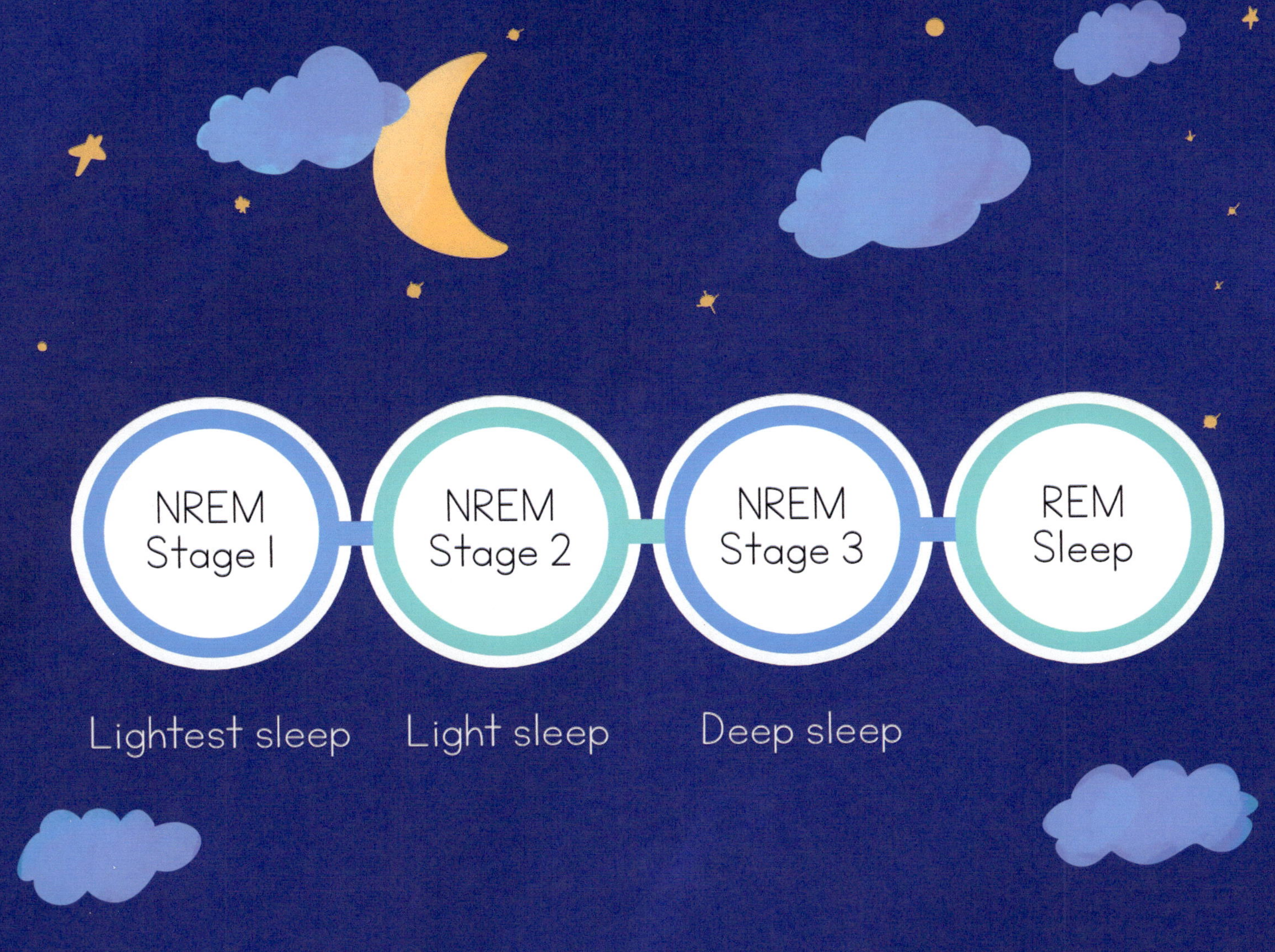

There are three stages of NREM sleep that progressively get deeper. During NREM sleep, our eyes usually have little or no movement.

After NREM sleep is REM sleep. During REM sleep, our eyes move quickly in different directions, and we can have **dreams.**

Nightmares are bad dreams that can wake us up. Although they may seem scary, nightmares are not real and can't hurt us!

Sleep cycle

Three stages of NREM sleep and one stage of REM sleep form one **sleep cycle**, which lasts about 90 minutes in adults.

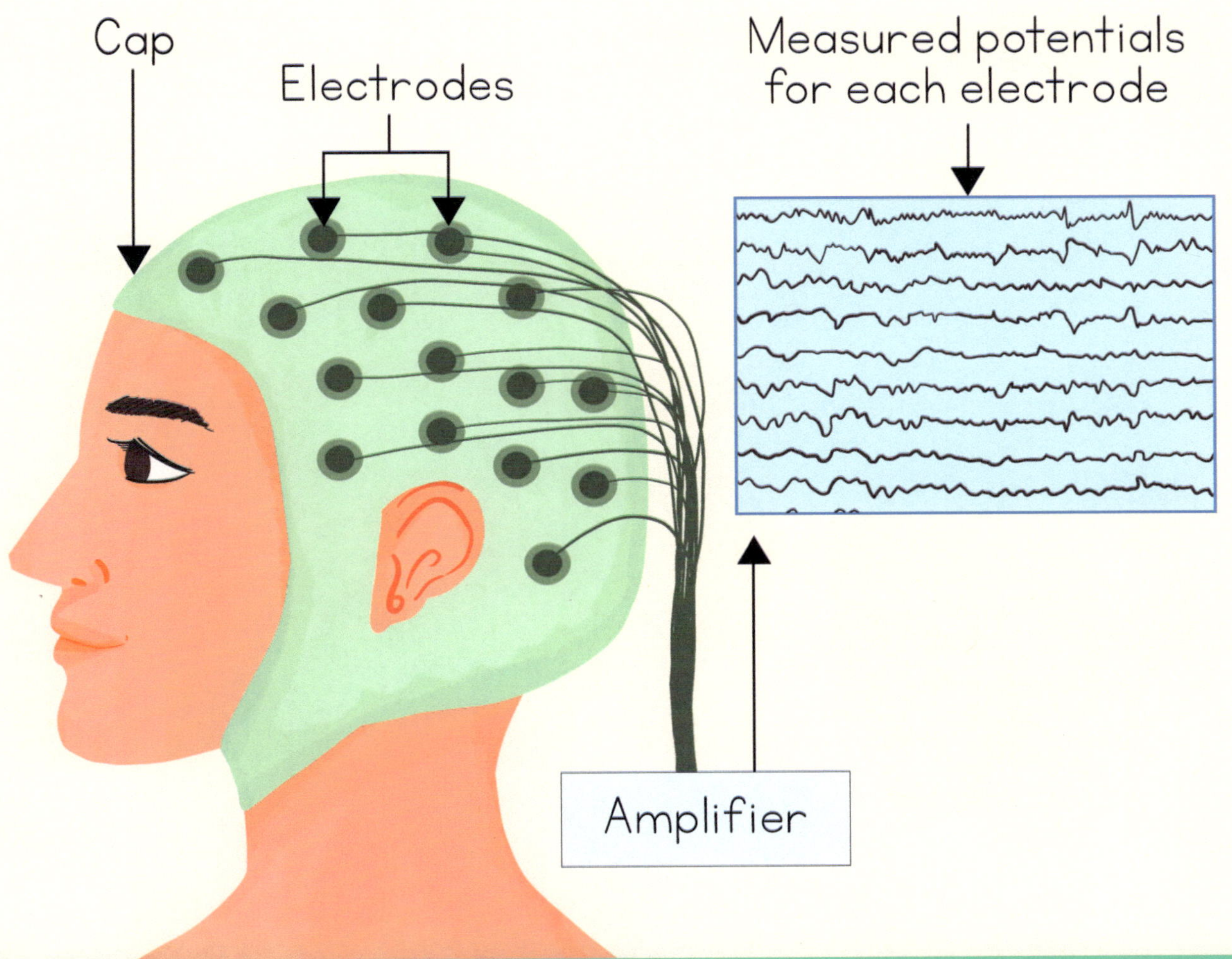

An **electroencephalogram** is a test that detects our brain's electrical activity, called **brain waves**. There are five types of brain waves.

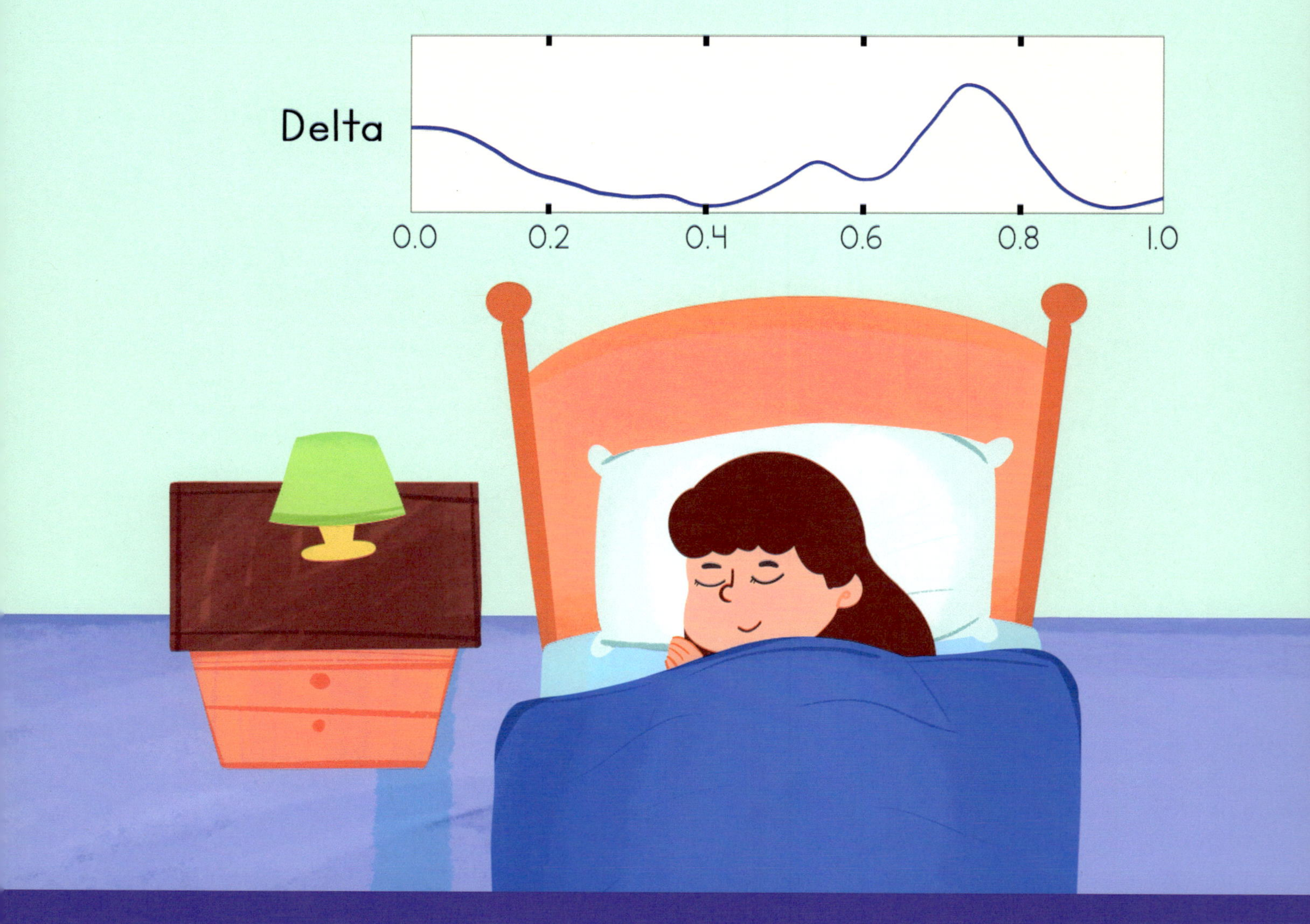

Delta waves are the slowest brain waves. They occur during deep sleep and are most often seen in infants and young children.

Theta waves are slow brain waves that are slightly faster and occur during light sleep or deep meditation.

Alpha waves are faster brain waves that occur when we are awake but relaxed, like when we close our eyes and take a break.

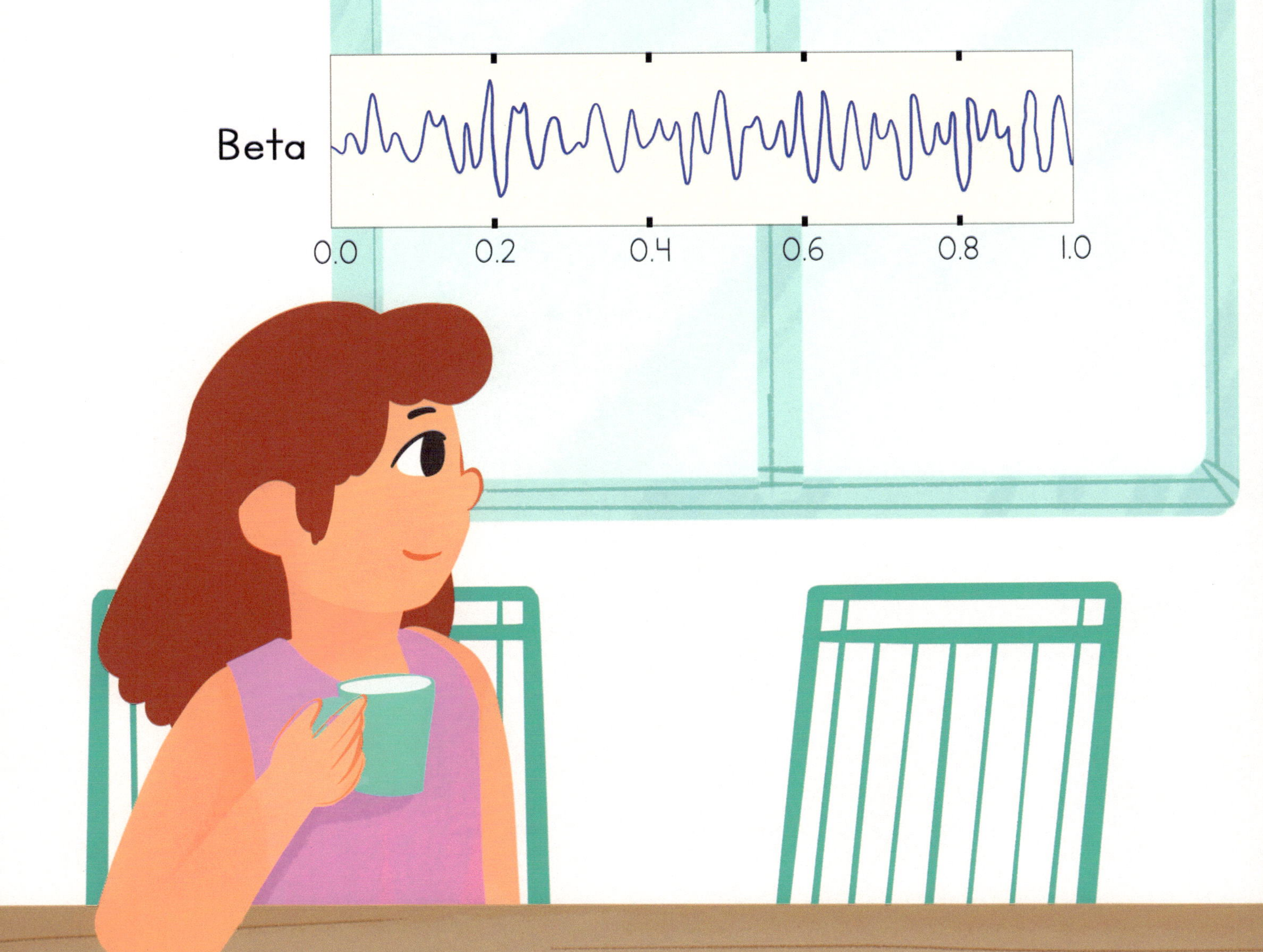

Beta waves are even faster brain waves that occur when we are awake, alert, and concentrating.

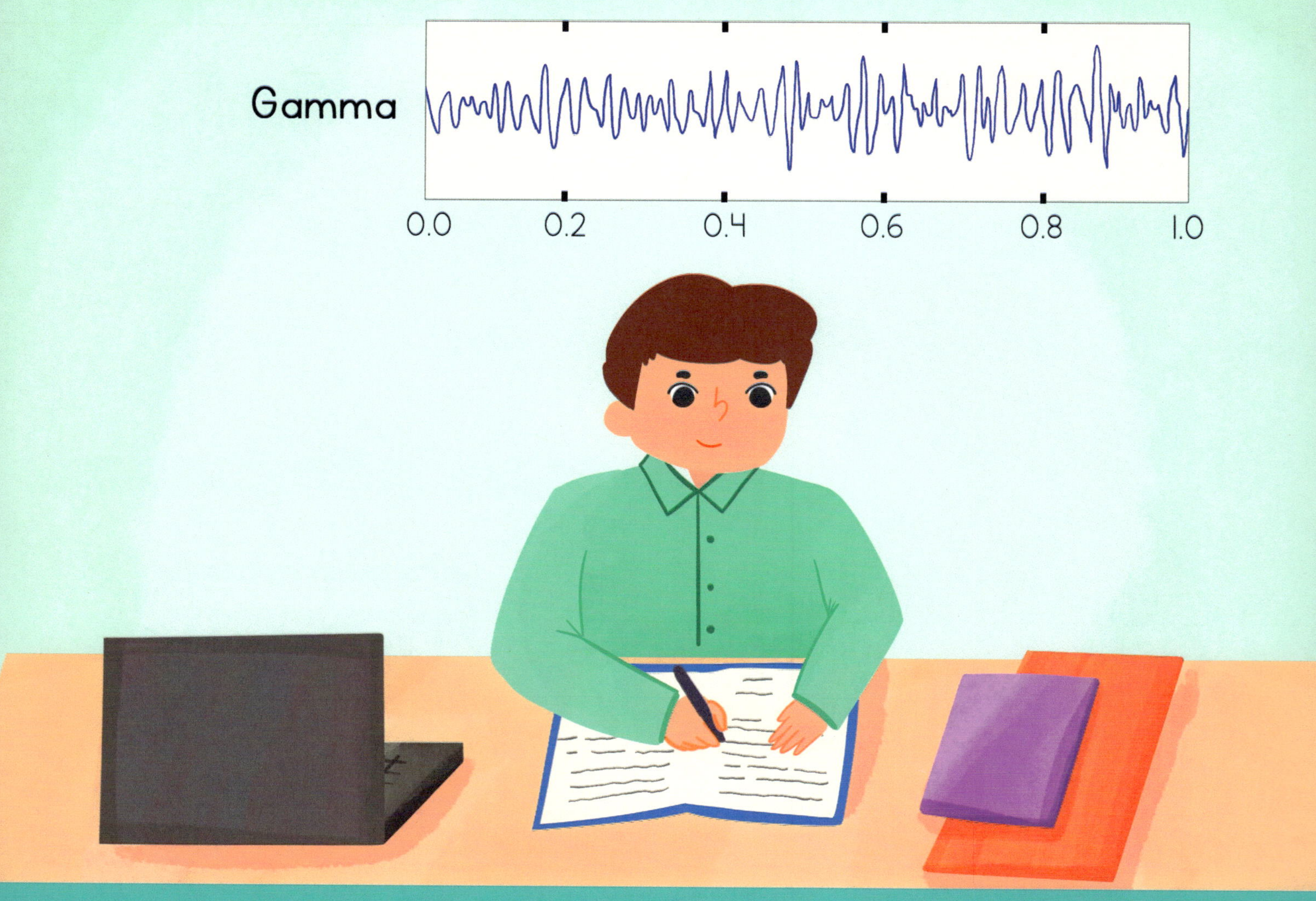

Gamma waves are the fastest brain waves that occur during higher levels of thinking, such as when we are actively learning or problem-solving.

Our **circadian rhythm** is our internal clock that regulates daily cycles of wakefulness and sleep. It is regulated by molecules called **hormones**.

Melatonin is a hormone made in the pineal gland of our brain that makes us sleepy when it's time to sleep at night.

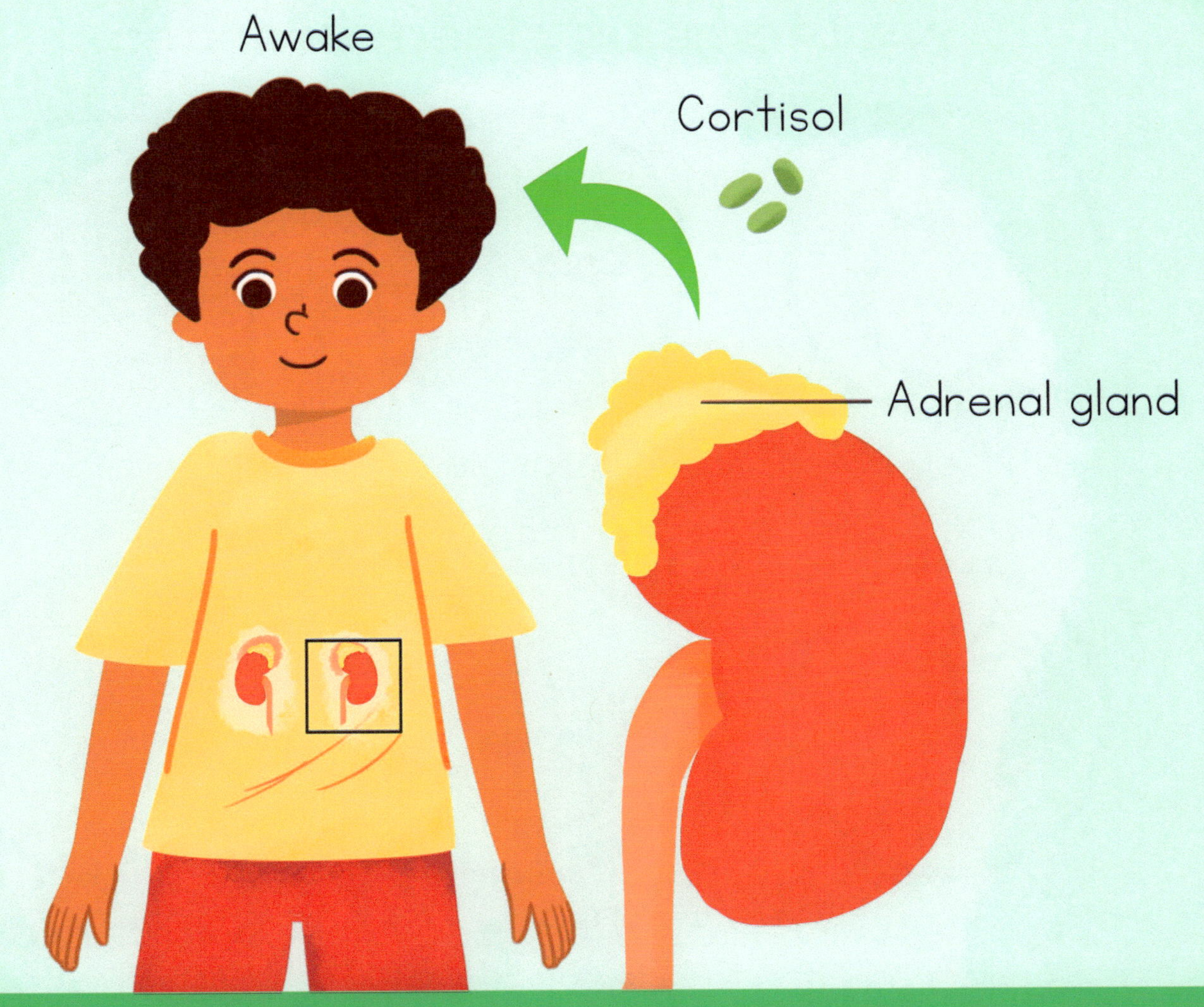

Cortisol is a hormone made in our adrenal glands that helps us wake up in the morning and stay awake during the day.

Symptoms of sleep disorders

Sleep disorders are conditions that disturb normal sleep patterns. There are many types of sleep disorders.

Insomnia is a sleep disorder that causes persistent difficulty with falling or staying asleep.

Narcolepsy is a sleep disorder that causes overwhelming sleepiness during the day.

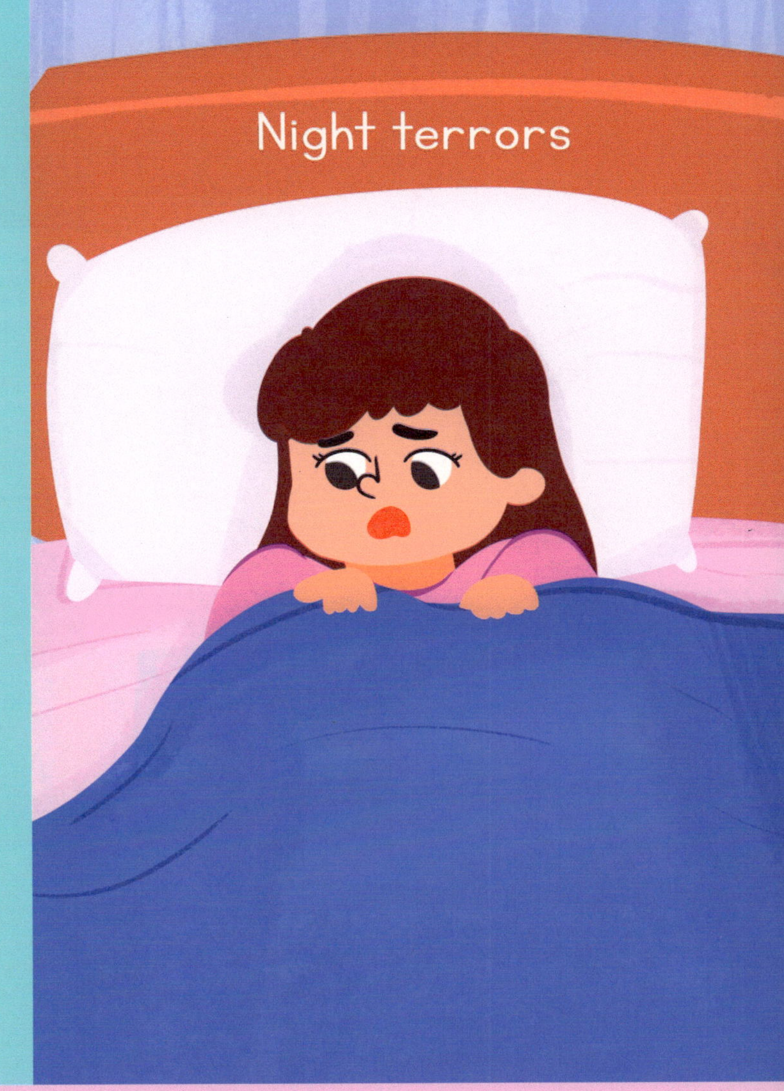

Parasomnias, such as **sleepwalking** and **night terrors**, are sleep disorders that cause unusual behaviors during sleep.

Restless legs syndrome is a sleep disorder that causes an uncontrollable urge to move the legs, often before falling asleep.

Sleep apnea causes breathing to stop and restart during sleep. It can be treated with a **continuous positive airway pressure (CPAP)** machine.

Sleep study

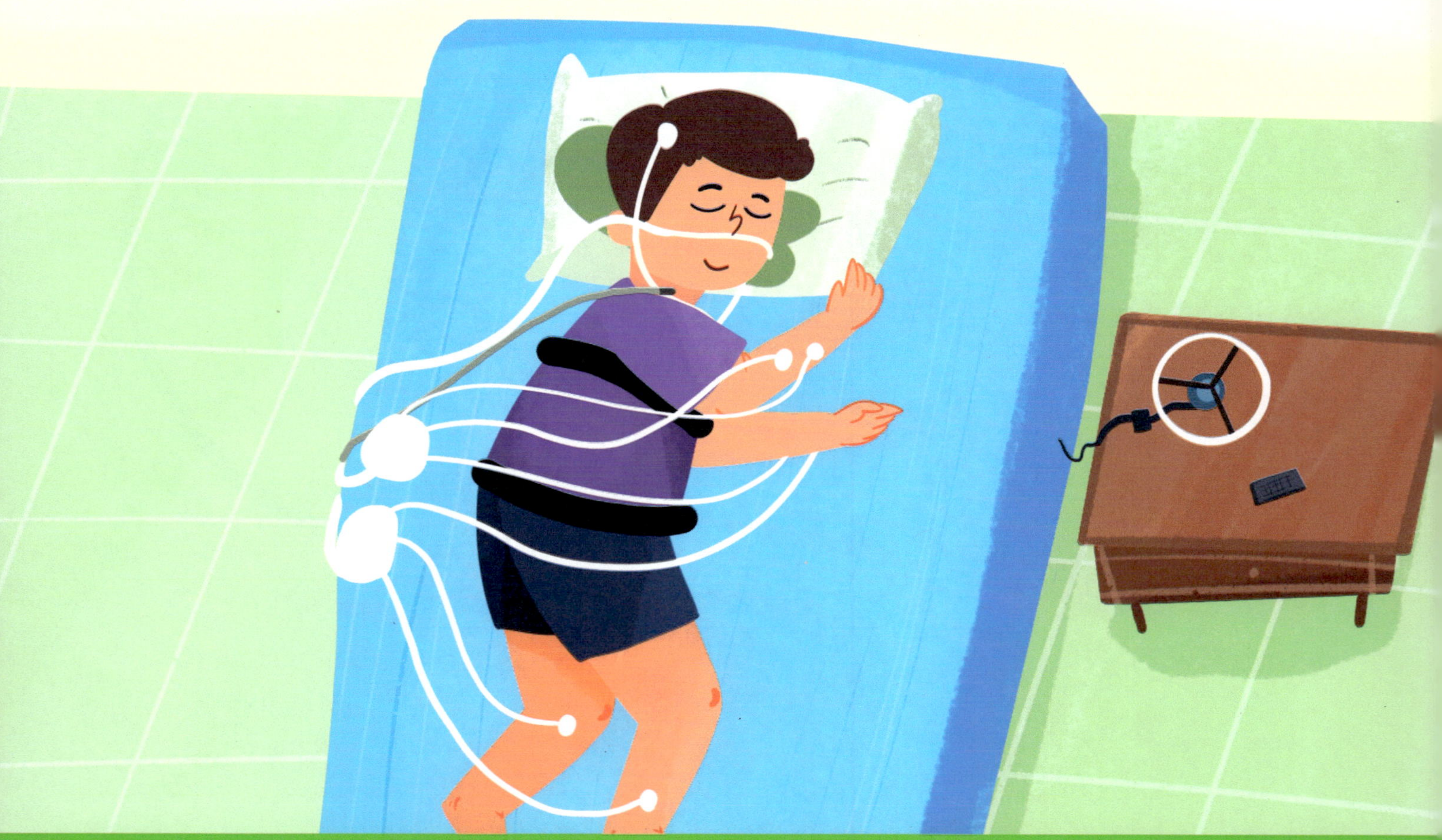

Sleep disorders can be diagnosed with **sleep studies**, which record brain waves, breathing, heart rate, blood oxygen levels, and movements during sleep.

Treatments for sleep disorders

Most sleep disorders can be treated with a combination of lifestyle changes, behavioral therapy, and sometimes, medications.

More sleep needed

Less sleep needed

The ideal amount of sleep varies with age, but generally, the younger you are, the more sleep you need!

A consistent sleep schedule, even on weekends, helps regulate our circadian rhythm and improve our quality of sleep.

Sleep is crucial for our growth, learning, and health. No matter how busy your day might be, remember to prioritize your sleep.

Every day, sleep medicine doctors help patients address sleep challenges and improve their quality of sleep.

YOU'RE A FUTURE SLEEP MEDICINE DOCTOR!

Glossary

Circadian rhythm (sr-KAY-dee-uhn RI-thm): internal clock that regulates cycles of wakefulness and sleep; regulated by molecules called **hormones**, such as **melatonin** (makes us sleepy) and **cortisol** (keeps us awake)

Electroencephalogram (uh-leh-trow-uhn-SEH-fuh-luh-gram): test that detects our brain's electrical activity, called **brain waves**, which include **delta waves**, **theta waves**, **alpha waves**, **beta waves**, and **gamma waves**

Insomnia (uhn-SAAM-nee-uh): persistent difficulty with falling asleep

Narcolepsy (NAAR-kuh-lep-see): overwhelming sleepiness during the day

Non-rapid eye movement (NREM) sleep: phase of sleep when our eyes usually have little or no movement; divided into three different stages

Parasomnia (peh-ruh-SAAM-nee-uh): sleep disorders, such as **sleepwalking** and **night terrors**, and that cause unusual behaviors during sleep

Rapid eye movement (REM) sleep: phase of sleep when our eyes move quickly in different directions and we can have **dreams**, such as **nightmares**

Restless legs syndrome: uncontrollable urge to move the legs

Sleep: part of our daily routine that allows our body to rest and recharge

Sleep apnea (AP-nee-uh): breathing that stops and restarts during sleep; treated with a **continuous positive airway pressure (CPAP)** machine

Sleep cycle: three stages of **NREM sleep** and one stage of **REM sleep**

Sleep disorders: conditions that disturb normal sleep patterns

Sleep study: test that records brain waves, breathing, heart rate, blood oxygen levels, and movements during sleep

Let's review what you learned!

1. What stages of sleep make up one sleep cycle?
2. What type of test detects our brain's electrical activity?
3. What type of brain waves occur during deep sleep?
4. What type of brain waves occur during light sleep or deep meditation?
5. What type of brain waves occur when we are awake but relaxed?
6. What type of brain waves occur when we are alert and concentrating?
7. What type of brain waves occur during higher levels of thinking?
8. What is our internal clock that regulates daily cycles of wakefulness and sleep? What is it regulated by?
9. What hormone made in the pineal gland of our brain makes us sleepy?
10. What hormone made in our adrenal glands keeps us awake?
11. What sleep disorder causes persistent problems with falling asleep?
12. What sleep disorder causes overwhelming sleepiness during the day?
13. What sleep disorders cause unusual behaviors during sleep?
14. What sleep disorder causes an uncontrollable urge to move the legs?
15. What sleep disorder causes breathing to stop and restart during sleep? How can this be treated?
16. How can sleep disorders be diagnosed?
17. What are some treatments for sleep disorders?

Your Answers

1. ____________________
2. ____________________
3. ____________________
4. ____________________
5. ____________________
6. ____________________
7. ____________________
8. ____________________
9. ____________________
10. ____________________
11. ____________________
12. ____________________
13. ____________________
14. ____________________
15. ____________________
16. ____________________
17. ____________________

Answer Key

1. Three stages of non-rapid eye movement (NREM) sleep and one stage of rapid eye movement (REM) sleep
2. Electroencephalogram (EEG)
3. Delta waves
4. Theta waves
5. Alpha waves
6. Beta waves
7. Gamma waves
8. Circadian rhythm; hormones
9. Melatonin
10. Cortisol
11. Insomnia
12. Narcolepsy
13. Parasomnias, such as sleepwalking and night terrors
14. Restless legs syndrome
15. Sleep apnea; continuous positive airway pressure (CPAP) machine
16. Sleep studies
17. Lifestyle changes, behavioral therapy, and medications

About the Authors

Betty Nguyen, MD

Betty is a physician specializing in dermatology. She was born in California but spent much of her childhood in Georgia, where she grew up on a chicken farm. Betty studied Biology at UCLA, where she was a Gates Millennium Scholar, and earned her MD from UC Riverside on a full-tuition scholarship. Outside of work, Betty is a certified yoga instructor and licensed scuba diver. She also enjoys journalistic writing and cycling.

Brandon Pham, MD

Brandon is a physician specializing in ophthalmology. He was born and raised in California. Brandon studied Microbiology, Immunology, and Molecular Genetics at UCLA, where he was a Barry Goldwater Scholar, and earned his MD from Stanford. He is passionate about medical education for students of all ages. In his free time, Brandon enjoys traveling, playing tennis, and performing card magic tricks.

Check out the rest of the books in our series!

Website: mdforkids.org

Instagram: @md.for.kids